GROWING

LEADERS

Roots of Youth Ministry Series

This series addresses ecumenical and uniquely Presbyterian youth ministry concerns. Volumes in this series are intended for both professional and lay adults engaged in youth ministry.

Series Writers
Rodger Nishioka
Bob Tuttle
Lynn Turnage

Series Editor
Faye Burdick

Titles In Series
The Roots of Who We Are
Surveying the Land
Dealing with Crisis
Rooted in Love
Sowing the Seeds
Growing Leaders
Growing a Group

GROWING
LEADERS

BOB TUTTLE

Bridge Resources
Louisville, Kentucky

Edited by Faye Burdick

Book interior and cover design by Pamela Ullman

First Edition

Published by Bridge Resources
Louisville, Kentucky

Web site address: http://www.bridgeresources.org

PRINTED IN THE UNITED STATES OF AMERICA

98 99 00 01 02 03 04 05 06 07 — 10 9 8 7 6 5 4 3 2 1

Library of Congress Cataloging-in-Publication Data

Tuttle, Bob, date.
    Growing Leaders / Bob Tuttle. — 1st ed.
        p.   cm. — (Roots of Youth Ministry series)
    Includes bibliographical references.
    ISBN 1-57895-011-2
    1. Church youth workers—Recruiting. 2. Church youth workers—training of.
    3. Church work with youth. 4. Christian leadership.   I. Title. II. Series.
BV4447. T884 1998
    259'.23—dc21   98–17979

Contents

Preface

This book does not stand alone. It is only a part of a larger series of seven books written by Lynn Turnage, Rodger Nishioka, and myself. There is much ground I don't need to cover here. *Growing Leaders* doesn't have to address the following topics and questions because they are addressed in these other books:

Read *Rooted in Love* if you're looking for

- devotional material for your leadership team meetings;
- inspirational stories of young people and adult leaders in action that you might use to begin your youth meetings.

Read *The Roots of Who We Are* if your leadership team wants answers to the following questions:

- What is reformed theology, and what implications does it have for our youth ministry?
- What are the five theological tasks for our youth ministry, and what are their implications?
- What are the five goals or intentions for youth ministry in Presbyterian Church (U.S.A.) churches, and what are their implications for our youth ministry?
- What does evangelism look like in our denomination in youth ministry?
- What is a Bible study model for youth ministry?
- What is the Presbyterian Church (U.S.A.) vision for youth ministry in our denomination?
- How can my local church write a vision statement?
- What are the young people in my congregation like, and what are characteristics of their age group?
- What is the Presbyterian Youth Connection (PYC) all about?

Read *Dealing with Crisis* if you're looking for

- a resource book that every adult leader should have to get them started thinking about how to handle crisis situations with young people;
- training modules for adult leaders on alcohol abuse, teenage pregnancy, suicide attempts, and suicide completion;

- a model for debriefing a traumatic event involving death or injury among your group.

Read *Surveying the Land* if you want

- a planning process for identifying the needs of young people;
- to assess the degree of youth involvement in your congregation;
- to set up a youth council;
- to understand what a balanced program looks like;
- a model for program planning that results in a balanced program;
- a broad look at places where youth ministry can happen, not just on Sunday night;
- a model for actively carrying out the logistics of a particular program;
- to learn how to communicate better with parents, youth, and the entire congregation;
- to examine how youth fund-raising fits into the overall youth ministry and stewardship programs of your local church.

With so many topics already covered, I can turn my attention to other areas that I consider important and can contribute to "growing" both leaders and a youth ministry program for the long term.

Acknowledgments

Like my earlier book, this book was also a tough one to write. *Dealing with Crisis* was challenging because of its content and because of the memories and experiences that it evoked. While writing *Growing Leaders*, I struggled with how I could keep the book a basic resource while at the same time doing justice to a vast topic. I settled on a blend: addressing basic issues of leadership training and program administration but then focusing a major portion of the book on a few topics that I could address in-depth.

Lynn Turnage, Rodger Nishioka, and I have retreated yearly to sketch out our design for a series of youth ministry resources that would be both practical and successful in meeting the growing demand for current and straightforward information. I had no idea how great a hunger there was for such help! I'm thankful for my colleagues' friendship and collaboration, and all three of us are grateful to Flora and Rick Hobson and their sons David, Patrick, and Cauley for their cordial hospitality in providing a place for our writing retreat.

I want to thank my wife Pat, my daughter Sarah, and my son Chris for their love and continuing support. I am truly learning from them much of what I need to know in this life. As I grow older, it is also much easier for me to acknowledge the debt I owe to my loving family of origin, who will influence me until the day I die: Daddy, Mama, and Diane.

This book contains two valuable styles of "covenants" that I gleaned, with permission, from Jim Kirkpatrick in Holston Presbytery and John Mayes at Covenant Presbyterian Church in Charlotte, North Carolina. Other forms and policies come from the operations manual of Black Mountain Presbyterian Church in Black Mountain, North Carolina, where both Lynn Turnage and I proudly serve as elders. The opportunity to put many of our ideas into action has been so very important!

Faye Burdick, our editor, has been supportive of our idea for this series from the beginning. She has prodded me to complete the task and has pushed me for clarity. It's been fun, Faye!

Once again I recognize the support that I've received from the Program Office at Montreat Conference Center and the insights gained from our continuing co-ministry here with so many fine paid and volunteer workers throughout the church.

◆ 1 ◆
Leaders We Look For

This book is really about "growing" adult leaders in youth ministry. Clearly, youth and adults should be working in partnership, but there are expectations of adult leaders to which young people are not held. There are legal issues that adults are expected to be aware of and that young people are not. It is also true that a number of good books have been published recently about youth and adults in partnership, most prominently *Teaming Up: Shared Leadership in Youth Ministry*, by Ginny Ward Holderness and Robert Hay (Louisville: Westminter John Knox Press, 1997). So I feel comfortable focusing on adults and their role in the youth ministry program of the local congregation.

This book at times may seem intended for the salaried persons in charge of youth ministry, or at the very least the lead volunteer coordinating the program. That could not be further from the truth. If you are the only adult leader in your congregation, or if you are a member of a larger team and not the coordinator, this book will be helpful to you as well. It will raise issues that you should begin to discuss with your team members—issues that will improve the quality of youth ministry in your church.

William Myers, in his *Theological Themes of Youth Ministry*, uses the helpful term *incarnational theology*. Although not a term exclusively reserved for youth ministry, its precepts do ring true as adult leaders work with young people. For me, incarnational theology helps focus the fact that adult mentors "are" theology for young people. Youth know who Christ is through the adults who relate to them. Youth try out various beliefs about the Christian life as they see it modeled in adults around them, even though these adults may not model this Christian life in exactly the same way. Adult leaders mirror theology and enable a young person to say, "Yes, I am going to believe what she believes," and, "Yes, I am going to act the way that he acts."

We look for leaders who exhibit the teachings of Jesus. This makes it paramount, then, that we look for adults who will take this mirroring seriously. We want adults who will struggle in their Christian walk to learn more about Jesus; they should want to "show" that Jesus to the young people with whom they serve. The Scriptures are the best and clearest place to look for the Christ, so I hope that adult leaders take the responsibility to study the Bible seriously. As I was looking for ways that other people "see Jesus," it struck me that the songs that we sing in church are chock-full of various images and descriptions of Jesus.

Take any hymnbook and look for phrases, nouns, or adjectives that describe Jesus. Here are some that I found:

- dayspring
- daystar
- enables you to stand
- foundation
- friend
- full of grace
- full of passion
- gentle
- giving
- good
- guardian
- guide
- healing
- humble
- kind
- leader
- light
- living bread
- loving
- never-failing wine
- rescues/saves me from danger
- rock
- serving
- shepherd
- shield/protector
- sought me when a stranger
- stay
- strong
- suffering
- sustainer
- teacher
- true

If we believe in incarnational theology, then we as adult leaders will strive to "show Jesus" to the young people in our congregation by being examples of Jesus in our ministry. Here are some questions for study, reflection, and discussion in some of your next leadership team meetings:

1. *Dayspring/Daystar:* How are we shining beacons or rays of hope in the faith and life of the young people? How are we pointing the way to the life Jesus led?

2. *Enables you to stand:* How do adult leaders help lift a young person? How do we help keep them standing when they are getting beaten down, when they are staggering under the pressures they face?

3. *Foundation:* How are we as adult leaders providing a foundation for the youth. How are we helping them prepare for the storms of life and faith?

4. *Friend:* Talk with some other team members, Christian education committee members, or session members about the privilege of being a friend. Now go down the roster of the

young people and ask the adult team members, "Which of you can claim this youth as a friend?"

5. *Full of grace*: We all make mistakes and need forgiveness. What are some mistakes that young people have made, and how have we adult leaders shown them grace? How have we adult leaders made mistakes and been shown grace by the young people?

6. *Full of passion*: At what times in our ministry and programming do we show passion for what we do? Are there other areas that need more passion?

7. *Gentle:* Do our actions refrain from being harsh and knee-jerk reactions? Do we refrain from any physical contact with the young people that cannot be felt by them as loving? Have we ever lost our cool and strong-armed a young person who was being too rowdy?

8. *Giving:* How can we demonstrate the "giving" part of our ministry? Would others describe us as giving?

9. *Good:* "Good" describes actions. Are we good? Are our actions good? Would others describe us as good?

10. *Guardian:* Adult leaders do not function as parents but as those who agree to take responsibility in place of a parent. Do we feel like guardians of the young people with whom we minister? What examples can we give of how we function as guardian?

11. *Guide:* How do we show the way to our destination? We are not the destination; we only help make sure the young people find it. In what ways do we as adult leaders keep youth from getting lost? How do we help them take the surest and safest route?

12. *Healing:* Who are the wounded young people in our group? In what ways can we be healers or at least be more aware of the wounds they carry and the issues they are struggling with? How can our youth ministry be a "balm" for them?

13. *Humble*: Do we always make sure that our egos are not in the way? What are ways that we can make sure that others, especially the young people, are getting recognized first? Do we recognize that whatever skills and talents we bring to our ministry are not our own but are from God?

14. *Kind:* "Kind" gives the image of a grandparent. Name the most troublesome young person in your group. What would it mean to be kind to [*name*]?

15. *Leader:* Leaders can be good and leaders can be bad. Being a leader usually just indicates that there are people willing to follow you, but it does not have a positive connotation in and of itself. The other phrases here qualify the kind of leadership Christ calls us to model.

16. *Light:* We're not talking here of light and dark issues but of clarity and discernment issues. How are we helping our young people to see more clearly how their faith impacts their life? Are we helping them be clear about how it impacts others around them?

17. *Living bread:* One image here is that of nurturing and nourishment. How does our youth ministry program nourish all participants? How does our youth ministry serve as "food" needed to live and grow?

18. *Loving:* How can we be more loving in the way we relate to the young people and other members of our leadership team or those involved in youth ministry?

19. *Never-failing wine:* Are we always there to "slake" thirst? Who are the "thirsty" young people in our group? How can our youth ministry be never-failing wine to them?

20. *Rescues/saves me from danger:* This has the connotation of actually learning skills that we may need to use to "rescue" young people, and also of responding to their plea for help. Which young people are at risk, and which have fallen and already need our help? Which young people are calling out to us for help?

21. *Rock:* Can we as adult leaders be counted on in hard times? Who are some young people who are going through hard times? How can we be a rock to them?

22. *Serving:* In what ways do we serve the young people and each other?

23. *Shepherd:* How do we lead the "flock" and keep them from harm? How do we watch over them? How do we give them green fields in which they can find nourishment?

24. *Shield/Protector:* Which young people in our group are in delicate situations or are on shaky ground? Which young people are being threatened either literally or figuratively? How can we protect them? How can we shield them?

25. *Sought me when a stranger:* Who are the strangers to our youth group and church? Which of us as adult leaders are taking the responsibility for making sure that strangers are welcomed?

26. *Stay:* Whether the hymn writer meant it or not, the word *stay* brings to mind the pegs I hammer into the ground to keep my tent in place on a windy, rainy night. I think of the lines tethering the hot air balloons to keep them from floating away every time the wind blows. What pegs are we providing to young people to help them anchor their own tents of life and faith?

27. *Strong:* The image here is not of physical might but of certainty. We don't have to be physically strong, but we need to be sure of where we stand and not be afraid to stand up for what we believe. Are we teaching the young people in our group to do the same, even if we disagree with them?

28. *Suffering:* What sacrifices are we making for the young people in our ministry? Are others aware of those sacrifices? Are we calling other adult leaders to join us in sacrificing?

29. *Sustainer:* The image here is of "keeping on, keeping on." How do we show the young people that our love and care for them will never stop? How can we prove to them that God's love for them never stops? How do we show encouragement during the rough times of life?

30. *Teacher:* What are we teaching by our words and actions? Do we recognize that whether we realize it or not, we are teaching even if we're not deliberately up in front of a group? If we're around young people, we're teaching them something. What is it?

31. *True:* Is what we say true? Can the young people count on the words from our mouths to reflect our real selves and not our fake selves? How can we be more real to young people?

Don't be like the men who questioned Jesus so strongly when he healed the sick man at the pool of Bethesda. Jesus pointedly told them: "You have never heard God's voice or seen God's form, and you do not have God's word abiding in you, because you do not believe him whom God has sent" (John 5:37b–38). In these verses we seem to hear a promise that if we *do* believe in the Jesus whom God sent, then God's word will abide in us and we will know God.

Later in John's Gospel, there is the story of some Greeks who approached the disciple Philip with these simple words: "Sir, we wish to see Jesus" (John 12:21b). I cannot tell from the Bible whether these Greeks ever got to see Jesus in person. Seeing Jesus in person is obviously not possible now. But there are other options available to those today who "wish to see Jesus." One option is the desire to know God through the believers with whom they work, worship, and play. In the end, the young people and other adult leaders with whom you minister deserve to see Jesus through you. What a high calling!

We need to look for a wide diversity among the adult leadership. Youth ministry is unique these days. The young people with whom we serve definitely come in many varieties! Although the young, handsome, male, guitar-playing adult still goes over big in some circles, the "pied-piper" style of youth ministry is gone for good. These days "it takes a village to raise a child," and it takes many different kinds of adult leaders who can appeal to and understand the young people with whom they come in contact.

We need as good a mix as we can get of adult leaders who

- are different ages
- are single
- are married
- are divorced
- are male
- are female
- are racially diverse
- are introverts
- are extroverts
- see movies
- watch music videos
- love sports
- enjoy the arts

seek diversity!

This is not tokenism; it is smart youth ministry! It means that adult leaders don't have to know everything and can share their ministry with others. It means that they can learn from each other and learn to respect each other. It means that this mutual respect will become obvious to the young people as well. It makes the odds greater that a particular young person will connect with at least one of the adult leaders.

Burnout is a familiar term these days. We see it in every walk of life, and we see it all of the time in youth ministry. The church is famous for taking advantage of the adult leaders by pleading with them to continue their ministry because "the young people love you" and "there's no one else who could do as good a job as you." In youth ministry that's dangerous! If we care about the adult leaders who serve us so well, and if we care about the young people with whom they minister, we'll be alert for these signs of burnout:

- procrastination
- depression
- lack of focus
- exhaustion
- lack of energy
- lack of enthusiasm for future projects
- irritability
- erratic behavior

} *signs of burnout!*

If there are adult leaders among your youth ministry team who show signs of burnout and who have had long terms of service, the best thing you can do would be to offer them the opportunity to take a break or retire. Encourage these people to serve the church in other ways. A private conversation can be arranged that might begin:

[*Name*], from what I've seen lately, it's becoming difficult for you to balance the many responsibilities you have and to serve as a youth leader as much as you do. I'd like to spend some time talking with you about ways to make life easier for you and still let you serve in a way that is meaningful to you.

Every time that I have had this conversation, the outcome has been positive. The adult immediately responded that I was right! It does take some inner strength to be able to raise these issues with another adult leader, but it can be done! A closing word: Don't confuse burned-out adult leaders with those who will offer to step aside to make room for new adults that are being recruited. Let them help orient and mentor the new adult leaders who are coming on board!

◆2◆
Recruiting Leaders

We need to define roles and write job descriptions. I have seen more adult leaders and youth ministry programs floundering than I care to count. Usually one of the major complaints is that no one knows who is doing what. At the Montreat Conference Center our department employs more than one hundred summer staff each year. Job descriptions are very important. The adult leaders who are being recruited deserve to know what they are supposed to do. But what most people miss, especially in a youth ministry program in a local congregation, is that there is one step that should be taken before writing the job description of the adult leader that is about to be recruited. It's a big one. That's why it is so often neglected. The role that each one plays in supporting and leading the youth ministry program must be outlined. It's the only way you know that all "bases are covered." It often leads to both a new understanding of the intricacies of operating the youth ministry program and a new respect for the role of each individual.

Sit down with your youth committee, Presbyterian Youth Connection Council, Christian education committee, or session, and brainstorm as big a list as you can of the jobs or functions that must be performed for your youth ministry program to operate. Perhaps you'll come up with some of the tasks listed on pages 9–13.

The possible tasks are listed, and the people who might have responsibility for those tasks appear below each task. Go down the list, taking one responsibility at a time, and look down the row, putting a check mark or names in the appropriate space. This is a great way to make sure that everything is covered. It also shows if someone's load is too light and if another is carrying too heavy a burden.

Youth Ministry Tasks

Communication and Promotion

1. Write and submit newsletter/announcements/publicity.

council

staff

teachers

advisers

parent

youth

short-term

2. Send out letters/announcements/reminders through the church office.

council

staff

teachers

advisers

parent

youth

short-term

3. Make sure that church calendar is up to date.

council

staff

teachers

advisers

parent

youth

short-term

4. Keep youth bulletin board up to date.

council

staff

teachers

advisers

parent

youth

short-term

Program

1. Initiate a planning process that will build a coordinated, balanced youth ministry program.

   council

   staff

   teachers

   advisers

   parent

   youth

   short-term

2. Recognize and celebrate graduating seniors.

   council

   staff

   teachers

   advisers

   parent

   youth

   short-term

3. Approve the budget request and fund-raisers for youth activities and supervise expenditures.

   council

   staff

   teachers

   advisers

   parent

   youth

   short-term

4. Coordinate youth suppers/snacks.

   council

   staff

   teachers

   advisers

   parent

   youth

   short-term

5. Reserve the church van for youth activites.

council

staff

teachers

advisers

parent

youth

short-term

6. Lead planning for conferences and mission trips.

council

staff

teachers

advisers

parent

youth

short-term

7. Connect our PYC to presbytery, synod, regional, and national events.

council

staff

teachers

advisers

parent

youth

short-term

Leadership

1. Provide feedback and guidance for the youth leadership team.

council

staff

teachers

advisers

parent

youth

short-term

1. Recognize and thank advisers and youth church school teachers.

council

staff

teachers

advisers

parent

youth

short-term

2. Recruit and approve new adult leaders for youth ministry; recommend those adults for approval to the session; train leaders.

council

staff

teachers

advisers

parent

youth

short-term

3. Keep youth advisers and youth committee "on task," making sure that details are covered.

council

staff

teachers

advisers

parent

youth

short-term

4. Assist in relaying pastoral concerns among youth and their families to those who need to know them.

council

staff

teachers

advisers

parent

youth

short-term

Now you can write a job description for the adult leaders whom you intend to seek. Using the information in the columns that you checked and what you know about the congregation and youth ministry program, try your hand at writing a job description that is no longer than the front and back of one letter-size page. Make sure that it contains at least most of the items listed below under "Job Description."

(This page may be photocopied for use with this study.)

Job Description

• What is the title or name of the position?

_____

_____

• What kind of reward/satisfaction can be expected?

_____

_____

_____

• What does the job entail?

_____

_____

_____

• What kind of training can be expected?

_____

_____

• Who are the colleagues or teammates?

_____

_____

• What kind of support can be expected and from whom?

_____

_____

• How long is the term of service?

_____

_____

• Where does this position fit in the "big picture"?

_____

_____

Now that you've painted the big picture and written the actual job description for the youth ministry leader, it's time to sit down with a small group of adults and youth who will keep confidentiality, pray together for leaders who want to serve young people to rise up in the congregation, and open up the church directory! Come up with a wish list of names, prioritize them, and run them by a committee or staff person to gain approval to ask the chosen individuals to serve.

Now for the most important part—actually challenging someone to take up the responsibility. It is not a task to be taken lightly. The person that you are going to challenge deserves the committee's full attention, deserves to be challenged in a private conversation, deserves to be informed as much as possible of the tasks he or she is being asked to perform, and deserves to have a short period of time to consider the request prayerfully.

If he or she says "no," then believe that God will raise up other leaders to serve the young people. If she or he says "yes," offer a prayer of thanks, gain the official approval of your session or governing body, and put the selected leader to work!

Growing Leaders

◆ 3 ◆
Supporting Leaders

This chapter may very well be the most controversial part of this book. Many of us are aware of all too many incidents where programs and lives of both young people and adults were shattered because a particular adult should not have been working with children or youth. Many governing bodies have been doing background checks on employees for a number of years. A growing number of them are beginning to perform background checks on volunteers, especially those who work with children and young people. Background checks create confidence in the youth ministry program and among adult leaders.

For your information, a sample background check form appears on pages 18–19. The company that Montreat Conference Center uses to perform background checks on both full-time and summer employees is listed in the Resources as one example. Other such companies can easily be found by looking in your phone directory under a heading similar to "Pre-Employment Screening and Research Services."

Performing background checks on adult volunteers with children and young people

- lessens liability

- acts as a deterrent

- creates confidence in the program

Although getting your governing body to approve a policy that all volunteers working with young people should have a background check will be a new idea to many, your current adult leaders ought to easily become allies, and so will parents. Ask anyone concerned about such a policy, "If you were a parent and had a choice, would you rather have or not have a background check done on the adults who work with your young person?" Here are a few ways to encourage leaders of youth to work in a healthy manner:

1. *Have a life.* As our lives fly by, we all wish that we would have done things differently. The longer we live, the longer that list gets! Yet you've heard it said that no one has ever heard a dying person say, "I wish I'd spent more time at the office." I often think that if it were rephrased". . . at the church" that it

would ring just as true! If anything, the true regret is just the opposite: "I wish I had spent more time with my family and friends." Can the term "well-rounded" be used to describe you? Do you have interests outside of the youth ministry program? If not, what are some hobbies or interests that you can begin to pursue right now? Make a list of these interests right now and be bound and determined to pursue them.

2. *Serve others.* Those of us in human service professions are all too often uninvolved in projects outside our own ministry. We rationalize this by thinking that we are working so hard that any discretionary time ought to be spent with our families/friends; we further rationalize that because our ministry itself is serving others, we have fulfilled our responsibilities in this area. While this may be true, service to humankind in other areas can be fulfilling, renewing, and refreshing. We may be able to take a week off and go to Mexico with our church youth group, or we may serve a meal once a month at our local shelter for the homeless. Either can give us a new perspective on both our personal and work lives.

3. *Remember, the Lone Ranger is dead, and nobody took his place.* If you are used to riding in on a white horse and solving everyone's problems, you may not have had an opportunity to look behind you as you charged about from place to place. You may get a lot of satisfaction rushing about from here to there, being welcomed as the hero who will take care of things, but it just may be that you are deceiving yourself by allowing that satisfaction to fulfill you. So you keep an eighty-hour week? So you have all the resources needed for any crisis at your fingertips? So you always know what to do? So what?

4. *Practice a more spiritual focus.* Daily set aside time for prayer, praise, and listening. Two resources for such times are listed in the Resources.

5. *Take care of your physical health.* Can you look in a mirror and see that you're a candidate for burnout? Do you look like you're not well rested? Do you look sad? Find something that can help you be happier. Do you look too serious? Find something to laugh about. These are not easy prescriptions, but they are self-evident truths. Notice that none of these prescriptions call for total 100 percent turnaround change. They are all minor adjustments that can help change your direction for the future in small, positive ways.

6. *Delegate and empower.* All of us have a million things to do. Although delegation may sound like "let me tell you what to do," it can also be thought of as giving others an opportunity to contribute to the ministry. Look at the list of things to be done. Which should be carried out by leaders who have the resources of an office and time during the day? Which are appropriate for an adult leader of young people who has time only at night and on the weekends? Which leaders have severely limited time? Ask some of these adult leaders to check with the young people to see if they are going on the retreat next month. Give other leaders an opportunity to communicate with the parents whose young people they serve.

Recognize the service that adult leaders contribute by taking time in your youth committee or PYC Youth Council to consider ways to flesh out some ideas for recognizing and respecting adult leaders' service. Here are some suggestions:

- Make sure they are "installed" at a congregational worship service or during a youth program.
- Ask them from what areas they "get their energy," and try to let them take responsibility in those areas.
- Have regular program evaluations.
- Debrief troubling incidents.
- Give regular recognition for their ministry.
- Engage them in regular prayer and Bible study.
- When the time has come, put a meaningful closure on their service.

Reference Check Form
Applicant for Volunteer Services
Authorization and Release Form

I hereby certify that the facts set forth in my application for volunteer services (and accompanying résumé, if any) are true and complete to the best of my knowledge. I agree that any misrepresentation or falsification of information, or failure to disclose information during the volunteer application process, may disqualify me from further consideration for volunteer work and, if already performing as a volunteer, may subject me to dismissal from volunteer duties. I authorize the inquiry into all matters contained in my application, and hereby give _____ or its agents permission to contact schools, previous employers, references, government agencies, criminal justice and law enforcement agencies, state motor vehicle agencies, and any other organizations for information concerning my background. I understand that all such information will be maintained in strictest confidence and will be viewed and used solely to determine my fitness for the volunteer work in which I have an interest.

I hereby release _____ and its agents, and all providers of information concerning me, from any liability as a result of such contact.

I certify that I have read carefully and understand the meaning of this release form.

_____   _____
      [signature of volunteer]   *[printed name of volunteer]*

Date Signed _____

Social Security Number _____ Date of Birth _____

Driver's License Number _____ State of Issuance _____

Previous Names

Have you been known by any other name or names besides your current name
(such as maiden name, previous married names, aliases, etc.) during the last ten
years? _____ Yes _____ No

If yes, please list all previous names up to and including present names. Enter
the year that you began using each name. Begin with oldest name first. Include
reversion to maiden name if applicable.

Name	Year First Used

1. _____ _____

2. _____ _____

3. _____ _____

4. _____ _____

Previous Addresses

Please list all previous physical addresses/locations of residence for the past ten
years (P.O. boxes are *not* acceptable) and the inclusive dates of residence at
each address or location.

Previous Addresses	Beginning dates	Ending dates

◆4◆
Overview of
Risk Management

Want to get scared? Sit down with a group of youth, youth advisers, staff, the youth committee, or just about anyone to discuss "risk areas" in your youth ministry program. It won't take long to come up with a long list! Here is a list I generated for you to start with.

During youth ministry time:

• Church property is stolen.

• Items brought by young people are stolen.

• Injuries occur.

• A vehicle accident occurs.

• Medical attention is needed.

• Sexual misconduct takes place.

• Suicide is attempted.

• A young person is lost.

• Alcohol/Drugs are consumed.

• Fighting takes place.

• Confrontation takes place.

• A young person runs away.

• A young person is left alone at the church or event after the rest of the group and leader leave.

Now add some of your own risk areas to the list. An incident in any of these areas may result in the likelihood of

• involvement in lawsuit;

• loss of support for program by church members and/or governing body;

• loss of support for program by church staff;

• loss of support for program by parents;

• loss of support for program by young people;

• loss of support for program by recruited adult leaders;

- damage to health (both physical and mental well-being) of a young person.

Any incident, particularly one lodged in any risk areas, has the potential to destroy the youth ministry program of your church or to demonstrate its stability and preparedness. Which do you want to be the case?

Of course, there is no way in our modern society to eliminate risk. It's dangerous just to get out of bed in the morning (and also dangerous to stay there!). Most of us just go about our merry way making our activity choices by weighing the benefits against the risks of that activity. With any luck, your leadership team has made the benefits of your church's youth ministry program well known. Now all you have to do is lower whatever risks you find in your program as best you can by establishing policies and procedures that address the risks that you consider to be the highest.

Develop policies and procedures that lower the risks of your youth ministry activities and show your preparedness to deal with risks. So what's the difference between policies and procedures?

- Policies are broad brush strokes that signal intentions and principles.
- Procedures are the checklists that you put into place so that there is actual follow-through on the policies.

Let's try some policy statements that might be drawn up for a potential risk area:

1. At least one adult leader should always remain at the church until the last young person has been picked up by parents or has driven away.

2. Every young person active in youth activities should have an authorization or a medical form on file and accessible in case of a medical emergency.

3. Young people should always remain on the church property for programming unless there is a signed permission slip for an activity away from church and the group is accompanied by an adult leader.

Procedures are the "legs" for the policies! So let's try our hand at writing procedures that can be accomplished and enforced. For the policy regarding one adult leader remaining at church, some of the procedures might read as follows:

1. Middle high and senior high adult leaders will take turns month by month staying until all young people have left and then will turn off the lights and lock up the church.

2. The youth committee will recruit for each youth activity one parent who will remain at the church until all young people are gone; that parent should be the last one out.

3. Parents will be encouraged to pick up the youth on time.

4. Adult leaders will be encouraged to end the programming at a regular time each week.

Design a permanent authorization form for parents. Why? Because it is the first step in making everyone aware that there are risks even at church! A sample medical authorization form is on pages 23–25. Perhaps there's a lawyer in your church. Ask him or her to draw up a release form that covers activities both at the church and away from the church. You might also suggest that it cover transportation in a church van and/or in the cars of approved adult drivers. Most permission forms should contain the following elements:

• permission to travel in van, bus, or car driven by an approved adult

• information on current medications and medical condition

• authorization to seek emergency medical attention

• notarized signatures of all parent(s)/guardian(s) (possibly done at a parents' meeting)

• understanding that the form is valid until revoked

Can any signature, whether notarized or not, actually release a leader or the church from being held liable in case of a serious mishap? No chance! If there is negligence on the part of an adult leader, your program is in for trouble. No parent or guardian can be expected not to sue if they wish. Their signature on a form will not legally prevent them from filing a lawsuit. Then why bother? Because it at least will show that you take the risks seriously and that you went to a reasonable limit to inform the parents of those risks.

The next four chapters address some of highest risk areas that I have observed in the youth ministry programs with which I am involved.

Local Church Medical Authorization Form*

Authorization Form for Senior High Youth to Participate in Church Activities and Receive Emergency Medical Care

Revised _____
[date]

I hereby grant authorization for my child/youth,_____ ,
to participate in youth activities sponsored by [name of church] Church until a
written withdrawal of such authorization is delivered to the appropriate church staff.

I grant authorization for my child/youth to leave the church premises under
the supervision of volunteer youth leaders or church staff.

I hereby grant authorization for any adult leader of the youth group or
church staff to take whatever steps may be necessary to obtain such emergency
medical care as may be deemed warranted. As soon as reasonable under the
circumstances existing at the time, a youth leader or church staff person will
take the following steps:

1. Attempt to contact parent or guardian listed below.

2. Attempt to contact alternate person listed below.

3. Attempt to contact child's physician listed below.

If the designated parent or guardian, alternate contact person, or physician
cannot be contacted after making a reasonable effort to do so under
circumstances existing at the time, a youth leader or church staff person is
authorized to do one of the following, if such is deemed warranted by injuries
or suspected injuries:

1. Call an ambulance.

2. Have the child taken to the emergency hospital by one of the
   [name of church] youth leaders, church staff, or other responsible
   person designated by any youth leader or church staff.

3. Allow on-site emergency medical aid to be administered by a
   licensed physician or emergency medical personnel serving the
   area where the aid is to be administered. Any expenses incurred
   in reasonable compliance with conditions set out above will be
   borne by the child/youth's family.

_____   _____
[parent(s) or guardian(s) signature]   [date]

Phone number: [home] _____

[work] _____

Alternate Contact Person: _____

Phone number: [home] _____

[work] _____

Physician: _____ Phone number: _____

Medical Insurance Company: _____

Policy Number:_____

Please list below any special medical conditions or allergies that should be known by youth leader or church staff:

_____

_____

_____

_____

_____

_____

[parent(s)/guardian(s) signature]

Subscribed and sworn to before me, this the _____ day of _____, _____

[date]   [month]   [year]

My commission expires: _____

Notary Public

_____

_____

_____

*Used by permission from Black Mountain Presbyterian Church, Black Mountain, North Carolina.

Medical Insurance Information

(please print)

Insurance Company_____

Address_____

City _____ State_____ Zip _____

Policy Number _____

Employee Name_____

Address _____

City_____ State_____ Zip _____

Current Medication _____

_____

_____

_____

List surgeries _____

_____

_____

List allergies _____

_____

Circle if you have a history with these medical problems:

Hay Fever	Cancer	Ulcers
Convulsions	Kidney Problem	Fainting
Lung Problems/Asthma	Bee Sting	Heart Disease
Allergies (e.g., sulfa drugs, penicillin, etc.)	Blood Pressure Problem	Diabetes
Other		

Illness:_____

_____

_____

◆ 5 ◆
Accountability of Funds

Your local congregation may or may not have an elaborate system for counting its offerings. Use your congregation's model for counting the money from fund-raisers for youth expenses. Build a few safeguards into your counting procedure to protect yourself and the other members of your leadership team.

- Keep separate the receipts for items spent for the event (food, supplies, etc.). The best scenario is that those receipts are vouchered separately by you either before or after the event is over and charged against the revenue account into which the fund-raiser money will be deposited. If that is not possible and you need to reimburse yourself or others out of the proceeds, you can present those receipts to the cashier and ask for a cash reimbursement. Each receipt should have written on it the name of the items purchased as well as the purpose for the items. Each receipt should be signed by the person who is asking for reimbursement. The cashier should put all receipts in an envelope and write on the front of the envelope the total amount of cash reimbursed and to whom that reimbursement was made. Then the cashier should sign and date the envelope.

- If there is advance cash necessary (e.g., for a change box), voucher that from the church and then return the cash after the event is over. If you have to provide the advance cash yourself, hand it with the cash box to your cashier and ask him or her to sign a receipt that you keep in return. At the end of the event, you can return the receipt to the cashier and get your money back.

- At the end of the event, but before any reimbursements are made, there should be a count made of the total cash on hand. This count should be made by at least two unrelated people; the count should be written on a piece of paper that is signed and dated by both persons. Then any reimbursements for advance change or for supply purchases can be made. A re-count of the cash should be made, and the reimbursements added to that, producing a reconciling statement that should equal the earlier count. At the end of the event, announce to the leaders the total gross and the total profit; this sets a tone of honest and above-board financial dealings.

- After the event is over (or while the others are cleaning up), take another adult leader in the car with you and make a run to the bank deposit drop. Keep the bank bag with the cash in full sight of both of you the whole time.

- At your earliest convenience after the event is over, write a full report of proceeds and reimbursements to be presented both to the church treasurer and to the youth committee or the church staff person to whom you are accountable.

If there is a sizable amount of money involved (e.g., airline tickets for a mission trip or national youth event), consider bonding the person who handles the money. *Bonding* is a form of insurance that an organization buys to protect itself against one or more employees. Usually a background check and other documentation is required before the insurance company will bond someone. The company will reimburse the church/organization for the misdeeds of an employee if he or she runs off with money. The opportune time to bond a position is when the position is vacant or about to become vacant. Have your organization pass a policy that when the position is filled, the person filling that position will have to be bonded.

- If there is a youth ministry checking account or if there are reserve funds, make sure that someone outside of the youth ministry program (perhaps the church treasurer or financial secretary) signs the checks. If that arrangement isn't convenient, perhaps two nonrelated adult leaders can be authorized to sign checks. Another safeguard is to set a ceiling amount (e.g., all checks over $200) beyond which checks must be signed by some adult other than the youth ministry leader. An annual review of bookkeeping is recommended. Here are some other dos and don'ts you may want to consider:

- Don't sign any checks yourself. Instead, voucher the checks from the church in a timely fashion.

- Ask for reimbursement only for travel/meals. Don't buy a lot of supplies out of your own pocket and then ask for reimbursement. Instead, try to set up credit accounts at reliable vendors.

- Turn in an accounting of money from trips and events, even if it is not required.

✦ 6 ✦
Sexual Misconduct

The church should be a safe place for all who enter. The lay and ordained members minister in the name of and for the sake of Jesus Christ. Yet we are becoming increasingly aware of growing numbers of young lives violated and faiths forever shattered by trusted adult leaders. More and more churches are establishing policies and procedures for their leaders who work with children and young people These policies and procedures will

- establish standards of professional conduct for adult leaders of young people;
- educate both leaders and participants about issues of sexual misconduct;
- assure parents and members of congregations that their young people are in trustworthy hands;
- limit access by sexual predators to the ministry of the church to young people.

There is no longer any need to recite the lurid details of cases of sexual abuse in local churches. Most church members are aware that this can happen, but many people still mistakenly think that "it can't happen here." This, of course, is not true. A compilation of research from insurance companies, newspapers, and lawsuits will show sexual misconduct cases that involve

- a male adult and a male young person
- a male adult and a female young person
- a female adult and a male young person
- a female adult and a female young person
- small, medium, and large congregations
- liberal, "middle-of-the-road," and conservative churches
- light, medium, and heavily populated regions of the United States

Anything can happen in your own church. In this chapter I want to lift up some of the most frequent steps that churches are taking to lessen the risk of sexual abuse and to assure their members that the problem of sexual misconduct is being recognized and dealt with in a faithful and professional way.

Enforce a "two-adult" rule. Yes, it may mean having to turn down a request from a young person for a ride to or from the church. It may mean asking another adult leader to stay late with you at the church until a parent comes to collect a youth. It may mean offering a young person who wants counseling a choice: either agree to visit with you and another adult leader or agree to meet with a professional counselor. If possible, these two adults should not be related. It may mean giving up a potentially great opportunity for building a stronger relationship with a young person by going on a hike. It may mean that if a young person wants to engage an adult leader in a long conversation, that the talk will be moved to a public place, in sight of others but removed enough so that it can be private.

Recognize that sexuality is God-given. All of us are sexual beings. God created us that way. So it should come as no surprise that in relationships between adult leaders and young people, sexuality is involved. Adult leaders should note that young people often have a heightened sense of issues of sex and sexuality. Therefore, as leaders you need to be especially aware of how what youth say and do communicates sexuality.

Jim (not his real name), an adult leader, pulled me aside while we were on a retreat at church camp. He was very agitated and wanted a private time to share a problem he was having. "Christy (not her real name) is all over me," he said, "and it's making me uncomfortable. Every time I sit down, if she's around she comes over and sits sideways on my lap. Sometimes she even puts her arm around me or lays her head on my shoulder. If I gently remove her hand, she soon finds a way to put it back where it was. I'm afraid someone will say something. What should I do?"

"Jim," I said, "I'm glad you're listening to your feelings about this matter. The integrity that you have as an adult leader of young people is a precious thing that can be lost in a moment, both with the young people and their parents. Christy wants to grow up. Her behavior, in many ways, is typical of her age and is to be expected. She is experimenting with intimacy, establishing relationships with persons of the opposite gender, and she looks up to you. You are to be congratulated that she feels as though you are someone whom she can love and care about. I don't blame her for wanting to grow up. But she does not have the right to grow up at your expense. These days, if an adult leader walks into a room and there is a young person sitting on the lap of another adult leader, that adult leader is automatically under some small cloud of suspicion. It's even worse if the adult leader is returning the affection.

"So I encourage you to gently extricate yourself from these situations. Here are some ways you might handle it:

- When Christy comes over and sits on your lap, give her a quick hug to show that you do indeed care about her, and then stand up and go do something (whether it's a job, an errand, or entering a conversation with another young person).

- Ask another adult to watch out for these situations. Take turns rescuing each other. If the other adult leader sees her sit on your lap, that adult leader should call her over to help with some task, to engage in conversation, or to throw a frisbee.

- Don't sit down while she's around!

"You can't anticipate every situation, Jim. All you can do is be sensitive to the issues of sexual misconduct and behave as best you can to keep yourself clear of suspicion in these matters.

Limit physical affection. "It's a shame," folks say. I hear this especially from female adult leaders who know how important hugs and touch can be these days to young people starved for affection. And I agree. But most resources today suggest a combination of responses that can still express physical affection, but in a limited way. Eliminate the back rubs but give more "high-fives" and pats on the back. Mirror the affection of the young person (if in fact his or her affection is limited). If he or she offers a handshake, don't offer a hug in return. If the young person offers a shoulder hug, don't give a full body hug in return. Don't touch a part of the body that would normally be covered by a bathing suit.

Do report any incidents. If you spend a great deal of time with young people, it will only be a matter of time until you are "caught"—caught, that is, in a situation that you realize might be misconstrued at a later time. You've tried your best to stay out of those situations, but it just happened. Maybe even though you thought you had rides all lined up after the late night event, there was no alternative but to take a youth home. Maybe you thought the church was empty and you were locking up only to find that a young person has returned to talk to you about something so important to him or her that it can't be put off until tomorrow. It has to be dealt with (or listened to) now. Maybe there was an innocent incident that others observed or walked into that might be misconstrued later. Whatever it is, when it happens it's important that you report it immediately to the head of staff at the church. If it turns into a serious matter, then from the beginning you have striven to make sure that the person you are accountable to is aware of the situation and given the opportunity to intervene or give you advice on how to handle the matter. Talk about all of this with your adult leaders and with other church staff. Make such reporting a routine matter so that adult leaders won't hesitate to report. Make it routine so that other staff persons won't think twice about it either. If the procedure is set up with the knowledge of the youth committee or council, then that awareness will be helpful to everyone. The advantage of the reporting is that it also helps you share the accountability for the situation with another responsible person. Be sure to report in writing, no matter how brief. Sign and date the report, and make sure that the text of the document addresses the person you are presenting it to. Keep a copy for yourself.

Such reporting is a good habit to get into, and it's one that may rub off on others. It may feel awkward the first time, but talking together before something problematic happens will make it easier. In fact, this ought to be just a small part of the much larger policy of keeping your team informed of the latest developments.

Establish a "six-months rule." It's tempting. An adult who has been visiting the church for a couple of weeks walks up to an adult leader and offers to help with the youth program. If your program is like most, there are never enough staff to go around. You may have taken up a number of folks on an offer like this in the past, but consider yourself lucky. Help your leadership team establish its version of a "six-months rule" right now, and get it approved by your church's governing body. Either someone on your leadership team has to have known the adult for six months, or he or she needs to have been a member of the church for six months. Let the new volunteer know that there is an established waiting period and that it's for everyone's benefit.

Hold each other accountable. It always happens. Every event of any size that involves both adult leaders and young people has an adult leader who just doesn't quite "get it." "Get," that is, the concept that these are different days and different times. I usually don't take action until there is a complaint or concern voiced. That way I don't overlay my own inhibitions and impressions onto the situation. But at some point I wind up having a conversation with some unsuspecting adult leader about his or her behavior. I usually try to do this in as nonthreatening a manner as possible, and I usually try to do this with another adult leader as a witness. Before I have a conversation like this, I confirm the behavior myself or from other objective sources, usually persons who are in a position to have witnessed the behavior but not persons who might have a stake in how the situation turns out. The conversation might sound like this:

[*Name*], I've had more than one concern voiced to me this week about your behavior. You have been observed [*I identify the behavior as best I can without naming the persons who voiced the concerns*]. Let me first say that this behavior does not violate our covenant at this point. If it did, we'd be having this conversation in another setting. There have been no allegations of sexual misconduct lodged against you. I'm talking to you now both out of pastoral concern for you and also to let you know that your behavior is raising concerns in our community here this week. These are different and dangerous times for both young people and for adult leaders. When you [*name the behavior again*], I can tell you that I and others begin to wonder if you are aware of the issues of sexual misconduct. I'm sharing this with you out of concern for your future service to the church. I'm sure that you love young people and want to minister to and with them. If that is true, then please hear my strong advice that you limit your behavior with young people and also with other adult leaders (at least while you are in the presence of young people). But I've said enough. It's your turn to respond, and I'll stay here and talk with you as long as it takes to help you understand what I've said.

Do they "get it"? Not usually. Do they apologize and promise never to do "it" again? Not usually. Are they grateful that I had the conversation with them? Not usually. So why do I do it? For two reasons: (1) because of my pastoral concern for both adult leaders and the young people and (2) because I've made it clear by my conversation that I and other adult leaders are now watching the leader and his or her behavior. I also hope that maybe, just maybe, such a conversation will encourage an adult leader of young people to reexamine his or her behavior and motives for working with young people.

Too much damage has been done to both young women and young men through the sexual misconduct of adult leaders. It is essential that we try to do everything humanly possible to prevent adult leaders from stepping into areas of trust and abusing that trust. In the long run, policies and procedures will protect not only the young people but also the faithful adult leaders whom we ask to serve in such vulnerable positions. It is another way of living up to our baptismal vows.

◆ 7 ◆
"Out-of-Bounds" Behavior

In every youth ministry program, the limits of behavior by both young people and adult leaders need to be defined. This is usually done by a decision-making group, is clarified by getting feedback from a much larger group, and then is ratified formally in some way by those who will be directly involved. This document is usually called a covenant. The word *covenant*, while not widely used in everyday language, aptly describes the contract or agreement that is made between all parties. It is a theological term as well. It would be good for your group to study the use of the word in the Bible (Deut. 4:31, 7:9; 1 Cor. 11:25).

Three Styles of Covenant

The three different styles of covenant appear on pages 35–40. I included all three because they contain elements that I consider valuable for groups who are writing their own covenants. A comparison of the three would be instructive as a part of the group process.

Dealing with Covenant Breakers

What do you do when someone breaks the covenant? Does some action have to be taken? What's the point of having a covenant? Who gets to decide what should be done? Who are the persons who need to be involved in order to make a decision? Prior to an event or trip, have a clear understanding as to who is to be consulted regarding such decisions. It may be just you. It may be you and a staff person. It may be you and one or more other adults. If the event is held away from the church, all of these people may be involved in the decision plus some adults "back home" via telephone consultation. In most cases, there should be two adults in on the decision. What support is needed in order for a decision to be reached? Get all of this straight before you leave on the trip or have an event. It will save a lot of headaches if something should happen.

Normally there are two options if the covenant is broken. First, if it was broken in a severe enough way, the bottom line of the clause "sent home at the parent/guardian's expense" comes into consideration. Was the behavior a severe enough infraction of the covenant that the young person needs to be sent home? Sometimes this is self-evident. If it is, then the decision about whether that action is practical and achievable needs to be made in consultation with the appropriate people.

Second, if the infraction was not severe enough for the youth to be sent home but does call for some response, discuss the infraction with another adult leader so that you know you will have the needed support. Then sit down with the young person, point out the good things that he or she contributed, but then say "you've got a minus now." There is "grace" here, but there is also accountability. Perhaps one might say to the youth: "The church and the rest of the group expects me to hold you responsible for your behavior. I expect you to do the same for the group. We want to come up with some contribution you might make that will be a plus in your behavior and for the group."

Depending on the young person, you may already have a short list of examples of pluses, like cleaning and washing the van, helping with grocery shopping, picking up trash, or taking an extra responsibility in some area. You may also have a list of possible minuses, like having the youth return to his or her room right after worship instead of going to the dance, writing a letter of apology, calling his or her parent(s) and telling them about the incident, or calling the pastor back home. This process also helps assure that there will be follow-through on whatever action has been chosen.

The choice is made. The young person has a preference as to what will be the consequence of breaking the covenant. Because the options were previously agreed on by both the young person and the adult members of the group, any option can be chosen, will be acceptable to everyone, and will be carried out. Everyone involved sees that the decision is fair, not arbitrary, and is the result of a process that applies to anyone.

Growing Leaders

Covenant 1*

Local Church Covenant
Youth Participant and Leader Agreement

Name of Participant or Leader _____

As a member or guest of [*name of organization*], by signing above I understand, agree with, and commit myself to the "Youth Ministry Covenant" and the "Youth Ministry Regulations," which read as follows:

Youth Ministry Covenant

As participants in [*name of organization*], we individually and collectively confess that we are created by God, and thus, are *connected* to one another. As Christians, we respond to our connectedness by seeking out the fellowship of the Christian community and by living our lives for others.

Responding to Christ's Call to Discipleship

As a faith community, we seek and practice God's presence in our lives through prayer, study, and worship, revealing God's love through action, words, and witnessing. Following the example of Christ, we practice compassion and forgiveness with others.

Responding to the Call for Inclusion

As a diverse community, we strive to be inclusive, sharing the good news of Jesus Christ with everyone. Taking responsibility for our own actions as individuals and as a group, we are accepting and supportive of all God's people regardless of their differences and our personal biases.

Responding to the Working Model of Partnership

As a committed community of youth and adults, we are all partners together, sharing equal responsibility for our youth ministry. Whether it is time, control, or personal comfort, as partners we give up something of ourselves for the good of the group. In seeking to increase and give value to each person's contribution to the work of the group, we also strive to build personal relationships based on mutual respect.

Responding to Everyone's Needs and Interests

As a caring community, we promote and support every person in their healthy development (physically, mentally, socially, emotionally, and spiritually) in order to lead them to the fullest sense of identity, belonging, and wholeness. While taking on healthy risks and challenges, individually and as a group, we rejoice in our successes. We also seek to support and challenge one another in our times of shortcomings and weakness.

Youth Ministry Regulations

In light of the "Youth Ministry Covenant" and in the spirit of partnership, we understand that the group as a whole will discuss behavioral issues in all cases (except where limited by a situation's confidentiality) during a called or a regular meeting in order to explain circumstances, share feelings, develop solutions, seek reconciliation, and increase personal investment and responsibility within the group. In these meetings every effort will be made to respond to each person as a child of God, include all points of view, build mutually trusting relationships, and meet the needs and interests of each individual involved.

Responding to Behavioral Problems

Any youth or adult behavior that threatens the values, spirit, or peace of themselves, others, or the group as a whole (e.g., violence, exploitive language, or breaking ground rules established at activities) will be responded to through a meeting between the persons involved and group leader(s) to discuss the issues and establish solutions.

Any youth or adult behavior that seriously threatens or shows disregard for the long-term health and life of themselves, others, or the group as a whole (e.g., any illegal activity such as stealing, sex, or the use of alcohol, tobacco, or drugs) will be responded to through the immediate removal of the persons involved from participation with the group pending a plan of action established by the group leader(s) in communication with the parents (for youth) or the youth committee (for adults).

Repeated poor behavior of any kind will be met with harsher consequences such as parent conference, restriction on participation, or legal action.

*Used by permission from John Mayes, Covenant Presbyterian Church in Charlotte, North Carolina.

Covenant 2*

Holston Presbyterian Church Covenant

Jim Kirkpatrick, Director of Campus/Youth Ministry for Holston Presbytery, wrote the following on PresbyNet in response to earlier queries about "rules" for youth events:

> What about no rules for youth events? That way there are no rules to break. This concept has worked well for me on youth events for both local church events and for the decade and a half of presbytery youth events.

> Instead we tell the youth to conduct themselves as Christians and if they don't know what that means then they should talk it over with an adult before they act. Then we give in writing and *read* to the adults the following statement as guidelines to help the adults to know what's going on.

> We have rarely had a discipline problem and never anything serious—it's all built on trusting relationships and mutual respect.

To All Adults

We are glad that you will be part of our community during the Middler High Retreat. Please know that our general rule for behavior is that we are Christians and therefore are expected to conduct ourselves in like manner. If there is any question as to what this means in terms of whether or not to commit a certain act, ask the director [*name*]. In other words, remember who you are and let your behavior be a witness to that identity.

As adults, your primary responsibility is to act as "adults" with Middler/Junior Highs, which means to lovingly help them to have a good experience. To accomplish this, we offer the following guidelines:

• Please know that you are the one primarily responsible for the behavior of the youth people from your church. However, you are also responsible to and for all others in our community.

• We ask that you help to see that all young people attend all the activities on the schedule.

• Be encouraged to participate yourself in all the activities on the schedule and strive to enjoy that participation with the young people.

- Be open to participating in the free-time activities with the young people.
- Regarding the cabins: A certain adult (referred to as the "cabin leader") has assigned the responsibility of seeing that everything goes well in the cabins such as observing "lights out." We expect you to help that adult carry out his/her responsibility thus also being a "leader."

If you should have any questions or opinions, please talk with the director of a member of the Planning Team. We are very glad that you and your young people are here and look forward to a really good time together.

With appreciation,
The Planning Team

[List all planning team members here.]

---

*Used by permission from Jim Kirkpatrick, the Director of Campus/Youth Ministry for Holston Presbytery, Kingsport, Tennessee.

Covenant 3

Covenant for All Youth and Adults
Montreat Youth Conference Covenant

(please print)

Last name _____ First name _____

SS#_____ Birth date _____

Group you are with at Montreat _____
[include city and state]

Where you are staying in Montreat _____

_____

For this week, we will be doing our best to live together as a family in Christian community. Family life is based on love, respect, trust, support, and spending time together. Each of us as a member of the family is very important. To create and maintain this atmosphere of family and community, we agree to the following covenant:

1. As guests in the township of Montreat, we will be considerate to those who live here by not walking in the middle of the streets and by following the curfew of 11:00 p.m. each evening.

2. As visitors or residents in the state of North Carolina, we will abide by state law, which prohibits the possession or use of illegal drugs by anyone and prohibits the possession or consumption of alcohol by persons under twenty-one.

3. As members of the Youth Conference family, we will

   • abide by conference center and college "smoke-free" policy by not smoking inside of conference center and college buildings and by only smoking in designated areas;

   • care for ourselves and others by not hitchhiking or accepting rides from strangers;

   • not bring skateboards, rollerblades, "super-soakers," or balloon launchers to the conference;

   • be responsible for our own belongings and respect the property of others;

   • keep our radios and tape players in our rooms with the volume low;

- not climb the mountains alone, after dark, or before sunrise;
- participate fully in the events of the conference;
- be responsible in our expressions of care, concern, and intimacy;
- especially care for and respect property in Montreat;
- respect every individual's racial ethnic background.

To be signed by the conference participant:

I recognize that I am joining this Christan family and community. I agree to abide by this covenant while I am a member of this community. I understand that if I break this covenant, I may be sent home at my parent's expense and my church session may be notified.

_____
[*signature of the conference participant*]

To be signed by parent/guardian:

I have read the Youth Conference Covenant and understand that if my youth breaks the covenant and a decision is made to send him or her home, it will be at my expense. In case of an emergency, I give my permission for medical treatment. Please reach me at the following phone numbers:

Phone: Day _____ _____ Evening _____

_____   _____
[*signature of parent/guardian*]   [*date*]

Please note all emergencies or past medical problems here:

_____

_____

_____

_____

_____
[*address*]

_____
[*city*]   [*state*]   [*zip*]

Note to Adult Sponsors: Registration is not complete until a copy of this form with all signatures is turned in for each participant. Forms will be collected at registration and held by the Youth Conference office. Please bring an extra copy of each covenant for your own records. Each individual covenant signed by each youth and adult will be collected from you at registration. Please place your stack of completed covenants that you will turn in at registration into alphabetical order. This is a new covenant form. Do not use old blank covenants.

◆8◆
Vehicle Travel

Should young people drive their own vehicles? Transporting the youth group is often one of the most challenging tasks of a leadership team. The temptation to let young people ride in vehicles driven by other young people is great, especially when there are few adult leaders. My advice is: "Just Say No!" Travel away from the church grounds is dangerous enough without compounding the danger by using young drivers. No matter how safe the driving record of the youth is, the statistics are against them. Youth events are often in the evening, an even more dangerous time. The youth ministry program needs to give confidence to parents that it will "do the right thing" and acknowledge the risks involved. After all, if adult leaders cannot even say "no" to this small but frequent request from the young people, how can parents and staff persons have confidence that the adult leaders will say "no" when the risks are greater?

Certainly it must be recognized that many of the young people do drive themselves to youth group meetings. Some even pick up their friends on the way or give them a ride home after the program. But each of the decisions in these cases is made by either the parents or the young people. That's fine. Negative answers need to be given in a gentle but firm way and in a manner so that growing skills of the young people are not put in jeopardy.

So the correct thing to do here is to put a policy in place, approved by your council, committee, or governing body, that simply states that in official programming of the youth ministry of your congregation, all transportation away from the church property will be provided by adult leaders. Case closed.

This brings us to depending on adults for transportation. There are two ready sources of adults to help transport your youth group: parents and other adult leaders. Both take preplanning. The longer the trip, the more unusual the time of the event, and the larger the group, the more notice and planning needs to be given.

Parents and guardians are often willing to support your program in small ways that don't draw them into large commitments of time or put them in proximity with their young person. This is especially true if they perceive that the independence of that young person from them during youth programming is a healthy thing. So ask them with enough advance notice of transportation needs and you'll probably either get a "yes" or "I can't this time, but call me some other time." Either answer is acceptable and meets your needs! Parents perhaps perceive that their young person would rather not ride with them. If that's the case, then parents have an opportunity to get to know some of their young person's friends.

Adult leaders are the second best source of transportation. I say that only because they already have other responsibilities for the youth ministry program of the church and also because they often better fit as "backups" to your transportation needs in case a parent is not able to come or in case a larger number of young people show up for your program.

What do adult leaders need to know about this responsibility? The responsibilities associated with transporting youth are common sense and serve to further emphasize that the adult leader is a role model for the young people in the car with them. Here are some reminders:

- Drive under the speed limit. A speeding ticket is *not* good publicity for your youth ministry or for the judgment shown by the adult leader.

- Drive slowly and be aware of road conditions. Driving at or barely under the speed limit often doesn't make sense if there are poor driving conditions, a number of pedestrians, or a large number of people riding in the vehicle.

- Keep the volume of the radio, tape, or CD down! Many adults (including me) are guilty of having volume up too high to be able to hear emergency vehicles, odd noises from the vehicle, or other sounds that might warn you to slow down and pay more attention. With the sounds inside your vehicle full of young people already at a peak, why add anything further to distract your attention?

- Fasten all seat belts. Most states require this in the front passenger seat, but you should require it in all seats! Again, it makes sense that with a car full of active passengers one would want to take every precaution possible in case of an accident.

- Don't take any chances. Don't let your passengers encourage you to drive in a risky fashion against your good judgment. The adult leader needs to be in control and thinking ahead at all times. Don't bow to pressure from your passengers to have more fun, to run the light, to take a shortcut and beat the other cars.

- Make sure that all drivers have a map to their destination. Then there is no reason to have to drive while trying to locate the right route. This also removes the burden of traveling in a caravan and attempting to negotiate traffic lights as a group.

Should adult leaders who drive youth have background checks done on their driving record? Of course! You wouldn't want to be driving with someone who had tickets for speeding, DUI, or reckless driving, would you? Neither would parents want their young person riding in that vehicle. Your council or governing body should consider whether a policy in this area needs to be developed that eliminates an adult leader who has a questionable driving record from driving a group of young people.

On longer trips, renting other vehicles often makes the most sense, even if it's definitely not the cheapest! It eliminates having to ask parents to go on long trips and it keeps you from having to ask other adult team members to put mileage on their vehicle. Some parents may want to drive their own vehicles, especially if your church reimburses for mileage (hopefully it does!), but common sense will also tell everyone that this is not a wise financial decision in the long run. Get advice from your church treasurer or from someone with appropriate knowledge about whether or not there is a need for extra insurance.

Perhaps at times your church borrows vehicles from other churches. This is often one of the most economical decisions. It also has a high risk. Make certain the vehicle is well maintained, and if necessary get it checked out yourself. Make sure that the arrangement with the borrowing congregation is clear. Who pays if the vehicle breaks down on the trip? Who needs to be called if there is a fender bender? In your state, what documents need to be in the vehicle at all times? Check the inspection sticker (if one is required in your state) and the license plate as well to make sure that they are current.

If you are using your own church's van, make sure that you or a knowledgeable person in the congregation takes the van and has it checked out thoroughly before you leave on your trip. If something is found that needs to be fixed, then you have a receipt to prove that it was taken somewhere for an evaluation. Be sure that this is done in enough time so that if a part or tires need to be ordered, the trip will not be delayed.

The more you travel in a church van, the more you realize the features that are valuable as you carry your precious cargo many miles. As you have opportunity to have repairs or upgrades done, or if the church is thinking of buying a new van, here are some features that can add both convenience and safety to your many miles:

- the widest, most heavy-duty tires available

- speakers for the audio system in the rear. This will let the driver avoid having to turn the volume up so high for the folks in the back seat that the driver's perception is impaired.

- dual fuel tanks to give a wider range and also to lessen the chance of running out of gas

- air-conditioning vents in the sides and rear of the vehicle for the convenience of the passengers. The comfort and perception of the driver won't be impaired by having the air conditioning blowing on "high" the whole trip.

- tinted windows all around the van to increase the quality of the air conditioning, to lessen the distractions that your passengers might provide to other vehicles, and to eliminate the opportunity for other drivers on the road to notice that you have a van full of young people and be tempted to interact with them

- rubber mats that can be easily cleaned rather than plush carpeting that will cause you to be worried about spills and messes

- an electrical adapter plug (or at least a cigarette lighter) so that you'll have a power supply for a citizen's band radio or cell phone

- cruise control, both to lessen the chance of a speeding ticket and to allow the driver to pay more attention to the other challenges that he or she faces

- no luggage rack on top. In my opinion, the vehicle is unstable enough as it is, so why add anything that will make it more unstable?

- no trailer hitch! Again, too many novice drivers don't realize how unstable a van full of passengers and luggage is. Why add anything to it that will make it even more so?

- a "backup beeper" like those found as standard features on trucks so that when the van is put in reverse, there will be an audible warning. This feature can be installed and paid for as a permanent feature, but it is often seen as a feature that is too expensive and can be annoying to other groups that might use the van. In that case, a simple solution is the purchase of a small combination light bulb and warning beeper found in specialty catalogs that can be used to replace one of the rear white reverse lights on your van.

- large side mirrors and/or a special plastic "magnifying glass" that sticks on the inside of the rear glass of the van. While these are features more commonly found in campers and trailers, they greatly enhance the ability of the driver to view the surroundings.

- an emergency first-aid kit, and not just a tiny one, either! Remember, you could have as many as fifteen passengers (depending on the size van you have), so make sure that the kit is well stocked and checked regularly. Make sure a flashlight is included.

- emergency breakdown reflectors. Here I'm talking about the large, sturdy triangle reflectors that you often see on the side of the road both behind and in front of tractor trailer rigs that have broken down. These are required by law for those vehicles, so you'll find them at most truck stops. They make sense because they protect not only your vehicle and other vehicles but also your passengers. The advantages are that they do not have batteries that can go dead, and, unlike flares, they do not pose a flammable hazard inside your church van.

- tire iron with four handles in a T shape. I have to admit that I've never had to change a tire on a church van in an emergency, even though I've probably put many, many miles on various vehicles. I think that with such great weight and bulk I wouldn't even try to unless it were a real emergency. But I've changed enough flat tires on cars to know that the tire irons that come with almost every vehicle are woefully inadequate. Most are one single piece, with a socket on one end that fits the lug nut and with the other end tapered to be able to pop off a hubcap. They fit nicely in the compartment with the spare tire and jack, but that's about all they're good for! If the lug nuts on the wheel have been on for a long time, are rusty, or have been put on with a power tool the last time the tires were rotated, you'll never get enough leverage to be able to get the lug nuts off. Then what good will all of your preparations have been?

How Old Should a Church Van Driver Be?

Twenty-one! There is just no reason in the world to lower that age limit. Make it a standard part of your policy.

There should be an approved list of van drivers for your congregation. Your church's insurance company may even require this. To be on this list, they should pass some kind of brief orientation and test drive. Not just anybody should be able to walk into the church office and ask for the keys to the van!

In many states there is a license category that is a kind of "chauffeur's license." This license is required to drive a school bus, larger vans, and light trucks longer than a certain length. Some churches decide to make it a policy that persons who are permitted to drive the church van have a "higher" category license. Everyone who needs to drive the church van has to study the section in the license manual on school bus safety, go to the highway patrol office, or take a special test. The result is a pool of trained, experienced drivers who are serious about their responsibility!

Maybe all these comments serve to make you hesitant to use the church van. I hope so, because I believe that every driver should realize the grave responsibility he or she carries when stepping up to sit behind the wheel. Responsibilities should be taken seriously. I believe that this is a much less risky way to travel than in cars with more vehicles in the caravan.

On pages 47–50, I've included two sample forms that include a van reservation form and a van log, as well as guidelines for van usage.

Van Reservation Form*

Date Needed _____

Time of Departure _____

Time of Return _____

Name of Group_____

_____

Estimated Number of Persons_____

Drive _____

_____

_____

Destination_____

_____

_____

_____

Reserved by _____

_____

Telephone Number _____

For Property Committee _____

Action _____

Date _____

*Used by permission from Black Mountain Presbyterian Church, Black Mountain, North Carolina.

Van Log*

Driver_____Date_____

Driver's License Number_____Date of Birth_____

Group Transported_____

Number of Passengers_____Estimated Mileage_____

Gas Used (What portion of tank?)_____

Was tank refilled?   Yes_____   No_____

Was van found clean inside and out?   Yes_____   j18

If no, explain:_____

Was van returned clean inside and out?

Yes_____   No _____ (This includes ashtrays.)

Comments_____

Please check any of the following equipment that you feel may require special maintenance:

Engine_____   Tires _____   Heater_____

Air Conditioner_____   Radio/Cassette_____

Interior Lights _____   Exterior Lights_____

Seats _____   Exhaust System _____   Windows _____

Mirrors_____   Brakes_____   Transmission_____

Other_____

_____

Comments_____

*Used by permission from Black Mountain Presbyterian Church, Black Mountain, North Carolina.

Guidelines for Van Usage*

The church van is a part of God's blessing to [name of church]. Its use should be to the glory of God in a manner that is consistent with our Statement of Purpose. Those who use the van should act as responsible stewards and adhere to the policies as herein set forth.

Eligible Users: All groups sponsored by or affiliated with [name of church] are eligible users. The van may also be used by other local religious organizations for local transportation *only* if approved by the Van Committee. The use of the van by commercial interests or for political purposes is prohibited.

Number of Passengers: The maximum number of passengers allowed by law for our van is [maximum number]. The minimum number of passengers that the van can be used for is [minimum number], including the driver.

Drivers: All drivers of the van must hold a valid driver's license, be at least twenty-one years old, and must register their driver's license number and birth date with the church office. Drivers are also required to meet with one or more members of the Van Committee for a short briefing of special controls and other instructions for safe operation before they will be allowed to drive the van. Drivers must agree to abide by the policies for van usage set forth by the session of [name of church]. Each driver is required to complete the van log sheet before returning the keys to the church office.

Priorities for Usage: Approval for use will be on a "first come, first served" basis. First priority will be given to [name of church] groups. If the van is not being used by a group sponsored or affiliated with [name of church], it may be used by outside religious organizations for local trips (less than [number] miles round trip) upon approval by the Van Committee. Nonmember groups must pay all normal costs of operation during their period of use. *The van should be returned with a full tank of gas and should be clean inside and out.*

Scheduling: Normal day-to-day scheduling will be done by the [name of church] administrative assistant using the Van Reservation Form. Reservations may be made by phone. Any conflicts in scheduling will be resolved by the Van Committee, a three-person committee appointed by the Property Committee. Majority rules (two of three votes).

Safety Rules: The maximum number of passengers, including the driver, is [maximum number]. Seat belts must be worn by all passengers at all times that the van is in motion. Drivers are expected to obey all traffic laws, including posted speed limits. Use of overhead luggage carriers and the towing of trailers are not allowed, unless approved by the Van Committee.

Minor passengers using the van must have obtained a signed parental permission form from their parents or legal guardian allowing the leader of the group using the van to obtain medical care should it be necessary. (The exception to this rule is permitted in cases where a youth is a visitor who is not a regular participant in church-sponsored activities.) Permission forms should be in the possession of the driver or group leader.

Operating Costs: In-house costs (gasoline, maintenance) of operating the van are to be charged to the van budget. Nonmember groups are required to pay all normal costs of operation during their period of use.

Cleanup: The driver is responsible for seeing that the van is clean inside and out, all windows are closed, all doors are locked, and the van is parked in its designated parking spot upon returning to the church. *If you find the van in a condition that is not acceptable, please report it to the church office so that your group will not be held responsible.*

---

*Used by permission from Black Mountain Presbyterian Church, Black Mountain, North Carolina.

Concluding Thoughts

Some folks think that leaders of youth are born with natural leadership skills, wise discernment, and a charismatic attitude that inspires young people. Certainly some adult leaders do seem to have such built-in equipment. However, in chapter 1, I brought up the term *partnership*—partnership between youth and adult leaders. In each chapter the partnership expands to the relationship among adult leaders and also the partnership between the adult leaders and the church. This partnership is defined, shaped, and nurtured through a youth council, a Christian education committee, and the session. This is how we grow leaders. No leader of youth should be placed in a solo act. Such an environment isn't a place of growth for either adult leaders or youth, but is rather a frightening environment of survival. Everyone agrees that our youth are important, and so are our adult leaders of youth. These leaders have a right to expect time, thought, and planning to be spent in enhancing their positions of leadership. Whether a small church with a few youth or a large church with hundreds of youth, the church needs to look at the components of growing leaders. When our church invests in growing leaders of youth, we harvest youth who belong to and have identity within the community of faith, and who develop their own leadership skills.

Resources

The following resources are available from the Presbyterian Church (U.S.A.). Please call 1-800-524-2612.

Dealing with Crisis, by Bob Tuttle. Helps youth ministry leaders decide how best to help young people and their families during times of crisis. (Item #095536)

God's Gift of Sexuality: A Study for Young People in the Reformed Tradition. Curriculum that addresses topics such as puberty, anatomy, physiology, sexually transmitted diseases, relationships, and decision making.

- Leader's Guide (Item #096210)
- Younger Youth Guide (Item #096211)
- Older Youth Guide (Item #096212)
- Parent's Guide (Item #096213)

Rooted in Love: 52 Meditations and Stories for Youth Ministry Leaders, by Rodger Nishioka. Very much rooted in the real-world lives of our youth and the culture in which they live, these meditations and stories are both relevant and deeply "rooted in love." (Item #095535)

The Roots of Who We Are, by Rodger Nishioka. Explores what youth ministry means in a Presbyterian and Reformed context. (Item #095530)

Spirit Windows: A Handbook of Spiritual Growth Resources for Leaders, by Ann Z. Kulp. A unique and valuable handbook written specifically to assist leaders in planning experiences that are spiritually uplifting for all. (Item #095537)

Surveying the Land, by Lynn Turnage. Focuses on how to build a healthy youth ministry program. (Item #095531)

For information on background record checks, please write:
Intellenet, Inc.
Pre-Employment Research Division
22 South Pack Square
Asheville, NC 28801
Phone: 1-800-280-9898; Fax: 704-251-0665

About the Writer

Bob Tuttle is director of program at Montreat Conference Center in Montreat, North Carolina. An elder at Black Mountain Presbyterian Church in Black Mountain, North Carolina, Bob has also served as director of Christian education at the Presbyterian Church of Radford, Virginia; the First Presbyterian Church in Spartanburg, South Carolina; and the First Presbyterian Church of Savannah, Georgia. He holds a master's degree in Christian education from the Presbyterian School of Christian Education in Richmond, Virginia. Bob and his wife Pat (also a director of Christian education), share their home with two cats, their high school daughter Sarah, and intermittently with their son Chris, a college student. Bob enjoys reading, hiking, and exploring the World Wide Web.